101 Leadership Actions

for

Performance Management

Ollie Malone, Ph.D.

HRD Press • Amherst • Massachusetts

Published by:

HRD Press
22 Amherst Road
Amherst, MA 01002
1-800-822-2801 (U.S. and Canada)
413-253-3488
413-253-3490 (FAX)
www.hrdpress.com

ISBN 0-87425-835-9

Cover design by ZenGator Productions
Editorial services by Sally Farnham
Production services by PerfecType

Printed in Canada

Table of Contents

The Heat is On!

There are probably few organizations in the world today that would not profit by greater performance management.

Whether your company has been impacted by 9/11, is a start-up operation, or is dealing with the impact of 9/11, attempting to revitalize a mature workforce, or wanting just to improve overall company performance, focusing on the performance of people is critical.

If you don't believe this is true, look at your company's or your department's budget. How much of that budget is designated for salaries? If your organization is like most, the percentage is far greater than 50 percent. How do you know if that money is being well spent? Actually, you don't, unless you document performance expectations and verify those expectations using performance measurement processes. That's what this book is about.

Don't let the size of this book fool you, though:

Performance management is a "one, two, three" task. Effective managers and leaders will tell you that developing and refining these skills is an ongoing challenge. You've taken the first step by picking up this book and reading this far.

Now step further into the book and begin the process of adding to your understanding about performance and the (at least) 101 ways you can improve and manage performance for your employees' benefit and your company's benefit—and for yours, as well.

Getting the Most
out of this Book

You don't need to read this book from cover to cover. In fact, you might even become a bit bored reading it from front to back, and doing this might not even provide you with the greatest benefit.

Our recommendation is this:

- Use this book as a handbook; lay it down side-by-side with the performance issues you are currently working on.
- As you encounter something you'd like to change or do better, check out the topical suggestions in the book.
- As you prepare to discuss performance with your employees, review some of the suggestions in this book for moving beyond usual approaches into other options that might be more effective.

- Get a copy of this book for colleagues or those who need some fresh suggestions for creating powerful short- and long-term results.

As you become more skillful in managing performance, use this book as you would a diary. Jot down other suggestions in the margins of the book that you have found to be particularly helpful.

Your life will be easier, and your organization's results *will* be better. To your success!

Get Your Head into the Game

Performance management is one of the fundamental ingredients in your company's overall success. When it is done well, your company is able to have the right people at the right place, at the right time, performing the right task. All of those "rights" are within your control as an effective manager of human performance.

Here are some typical attitudes toward performance management. Which one fits you?

- [ ] It's a necessary evil.
- [ ] I wouldn't do it if I didn't have to.
- [ ] Some days I'm better at it than others.
- [ ] I don't like getting in people's faces about their performance.
- [ ] I'd rather just get good people and have them do their thing.

☐ I'll do it because the company says so.
☐ There are some things I do well and others I can improve upon.
☐ I see myself getting better at this.

If you checked any one of the first six boxes, it might be time for you to reconsider your attitude toward performance management. As you do, you'll find that your team will improve—and you will as well.

Let's get started!

1

Define what performance management is all about.

Why does your organization appraise performance? Why should you? What is the carrot that would motivate *you* to do a good job? What is the stick that you would want to avoid using for poor performance?

2

Determine your purpose for managing performance.

The organization's carrot and stick approach will get you going, but ultimately you should manage performance because you fully understand that it is part of your role as an effective leader in the organization. For what specific reasons do you want to make sure your employees' performance is well-managed? Keep this rationale in front of you (tattoo it on your forehead, if you must).

3

Identify your current level of effectiveness.

Use a scale of 1–10 (where 1 is low and 10 is high) to assess how effectively you currently manage your employees' performance. Be as realistic as possible. Since this assessment is just for your information, be completely honest.

4

Determine where on that scale you'd like to be.

If you're going to improve, part of the reason (hopefully a significant part) should be because you see some gap between where you are performance-wise and where you would like to be, and you wish to close this performance gap.

This information can help you formulate your personal goal to manage performance more effectively.

5

Ask others to evaluate your effectiveness.

You might be a new manager or you might have managed for 40 years. If you are a seasoned manager, ask several previous appraisees to evaluate your effectiveness. Identify people whom you know will be totally honest—you get no points for deception!

6

Ask others where they believe you should be.

A few of those same honest people will likely let you know where they believe your performance should be—and they might even be so generous as to offer specific suggestions on how you can improve. Listen to them. Take notes, and as you go through the performance year, make it a point to incorporate some of their suggestions into what you are doing.

7

Performance management occurs in three phases.

During the remainder of this handbook, we'll be exploring the three phases of effective performance management: those things that occur **before the appraisal** (preparation stuff); the things that occur **during the appraisal** (the eyeball-to-eyeball stuff); and the things that occur **after the appraisal** (the things that will set the stage for employee growth and the next stage of your performance coaching).

Knowing that there are three stages might lead you to think that one stage is more important than another. Resist that temptation! All three of the stages are vitally important to ensuring that your employees' performance is in alignment with your organization's needs and in alignment with your expectations as a leader.

As you review these three stages, set specific developmental goals for yourself. Although performance management addresses your employees' needs, it also addresses your needs as a leader. Make this a time where you are also learning, growing, and improving your performance in every one of the phases.

Before the Appraisal

Part of the reason so many managers despise doing performance appraisals is because the process of appraising performance, in their minds, begins and ends with the appraisal document—the thing you often have to send to human resources. Wrong!

If you are guilty of having this perspective, we would like to offer you a comparison: Let's suppose that you are going to pay your annual income taxes (a task we highly recommend). In general, you know that this task occurs every April 15th, right? You might get a reprieve if the 15th falls on the weekend, but if you're someone who waits until the last minute (and you have a lot of company), the 15th is your date. If you know this sacred U.S. event is about to occur, at what point would you begin to prepare (you know, collecting receipts, tracking potential deductions, and the like)? Would you wait until April 14th? If so, buy another copy of this book. You'll need it!

Our approach is a bit more stress-free: *Start early!* Whether you are planning to pay on your taxes (or receive a refund) or you are seeking to get your employees' appraisals done on time, your life will be qualitatively better if you take the time to do the necessary up-front work before you sit down to complete the final document.

And this "up-front" work is not overly time consuming. For the most part, you can get it done in 15 minutes or less. When you're finished, those 15 minutes will feel as if they added years to your life—and life to your years!

8

Make sure your employees know what is expected of them.

Simple, huh? You would be surprised at the number of times employees report that they have no clue as to what their supervisors expect of them. Letting employees know what's expected of them does not have to be an overwhelming task—it can simply consist of a list of tasks and duties that they should perform. It can also be a more formal description of their position roles and responsibilities.

9

Clarify and document the most important goals.

One of the greatest points of disconnects between employees and supervisors occurs because those things that are perceived to be most important are not written down. As a result, confusion abounds. Save yourself time and grief: Write down the most important goals. Then share them.

10

Make sure every employee has a set of goals.

Every one of your employees should have his or her own set of goals. Even if employee roles are the same, give each person their own copy of the most essential goals—and make sure they understand what they entail.

11

Make sure that these goals are SMART.

SMART stands for Specific, Measurable, Attainable with challenge, Realistic, and Timely.

This simple acronym will help you and your employees create goals that will ultimately sharpen focus and enhance the likelihood of goal achievement.

12

Meet with everyone in your organization to review objectives.

Pull together everyone who works in your organization and review the goals that the team is committed to achieving. This will ensure that all your employees are aware of the goals of their colleagues and minimize the risk of conflicting goals. If you encourage teamwork, goals will facilitate such collaboration in the areas that are most critical to your success.

13

Make sure employees know **what and how.**

Knowing the *what* of goals is critical, but knowing *how* is even more important. The *how* will set your employees on a course that will enable laser-like focus. If your employees are confused about what they need to do, clarify the specifics.

14

Encourage effective employee teamwork.

Employee goals should be reviewed individually, but be sure to emphasize why it is important for employees to work together to achieve goals. This will enable cross-training and coaching, as well as facilitate a higher level of satisfaction with work.

15

Develop and maintain a "drop file" for each employee.

Create a "drop file" that includes notes from supervisors, letters, and other items relative to each employee's performance. This drop file will be a tremendous resource as you collect information important for your employees' annual appraisals.

16

Add to employees' drop files at least monthly.

By keeping the drop file reasonably up-to-date, you will not run the risk of having a lopsided appraisal—an appraisal that is focused on only one area of performance. You'll also avoid the pitfall of having information from only a very limited part of the performance year.

17

Inform your employees of your drop file.

Invite them to review the contents periodically (this will minimize the shock factor at the time of the appraisal). Pay attention to your employees' re-action as they review their files, should they choose to do so. It might be necessary to coach your em-ployees about how to effectively respond to feed-back as a result of this action.

18

Request feedback from other key individuals.

Rather than waiting until the end of the year, request regular feedback from those with whom your employees work. This will avoid the "recency effect" that comes about as a result of giving feedback only on events that occurred in recent time periods.

19

Include feedback in each employee's drop file.

As you give employees feedback about their performance, make notes of that feedback (even Post-it notes will do). Then place these notes in the employee's drop file.

Make sure you use the drop file regularly. It will be a great time saver and a useful resource to you at appraisal time.

20

Develop a survey to gather information.

If you have access to help from the training and development staff, enlist their help in producing a survey that can provide you with more information on your employees' performance (especially if their work requires them to support individuals outside of your work group).

21

Gather production reports and other indicators.

If your organization generates production reports, make sure you retain the data that is relevant to your employees. Stash this information in binders or in some other storage space that is easily accessible. If you are able to retain this information electronically, this is even better.

22

Capture comments on employee performance.

Casual comments about your employees' performance also provide a source of potential data for the appraisal. As you receive these comments (over lunch, in other meetings, in the hallway), make sure you document these comments in the employee's drop file.

23

Review every employee's file to make sure it is balanced.

At least once each quarter, review your employee files to make sure that the data contained in the file represents a balance. Is the data overwhelmingly positive? Overwhelmingly negative? Make sure you have the information on where the employee has performed well, as well as the information that shows where improvement is needed.

24

Gather a wide array of information for each employee's drop file.

Newspaper articles, company newsletters, and other kinds of information about the employee's work can paint a fairly accurate picture of how well the employee performed over the course of the year.

25

Hold periodic meetings with your employees.

Try to meet with each employee at least quarterly if schedule and availability allow (more often is even better). The purpose of these meetings is to hold a dialogue with your employees regarding their current performance.

26

Give your employees honest feedback.

Before the meeting begins, determine that you're going to give honest and straightforward feedback. If necessary, have a trusted colleague help you rehearse. He or she can give you feedback on the impact of your statements.

27

Let employees know what you see as their strengths.

Even the worst employees are likely to have one or two things that they do well. Make sure you're aware of their strengths, and start by reviewing them. This will help to create a positive environment and actually reinforce the employees' commitment to improve.

28

Clarify how the employee's strengths can help improve weaker areas.

Your employee will likely have areas where improvement is needed. Which strengths can be used to address those weaker areas? Brainstorm those possibilities with your employee and come up with a game plan that will leverage the employee's strengths to deal with his or her weaknesses.

29

Modify goals to reflect current realities.

Business needs will change as the year progresses. Some things will become more important, while other things will diminish in importance. Make sure that all your employees work from a set of goals that reflect current realities.

30

Solicit feedback from others.

Identify present or past colleagues who can give you feedback on the employee's effectiveness, such as teammates and people who have worked on projects with the employee. Anyone who has interacted with them should be encouraged to provide feedback.

31

Encourage employees to network.

Addressing performance deficiencies is often a multi-faceted process. One often overlooked means of improving an employee's performance is to have them work with someone who is considered an "expert" in the target area. Networking is a good way to forge such relationships.

32

Ask employees what you can do to help them.

You might be able to help the employee with his or her performance problems. ASK! And don't ignore the need to provide regular encouragement and morale building.

33

Identify the point in time when performance started to decline.

Make sure you know when performance started to slip. Note the events surrounding the performance decline. Was there a change in the systems or in the structure of the job? Was there a change in work hours or conditions? What's different?

34

Discuss the performance decline with the employee.

What does the employee see as the reason for the performance decline? Try to help him or her identify the cause of the decline and ways to go about reversing it.

35

Celebrate milestones toward goal achievement.

Strengthening some weak areas will be a long and slow process, and the employee's confidence and enthusiasm will begin to lag after a period of time. Make sure those small achievements are recognized.

36

Keep a stash of small rewards.

We all need a pat on the back now and then. When employees in your work group reach a milestone or simply need to know they're on track, they will appreciate and respond to small rewards such as coupons to fast food restaurants, movie tickets, and items that are fun and of relatively small value.

37

Recognize major employee accomplishments.

Recognition is one of the areas on which supervisors score the lowest on employee surveys. Identify ways to recognize your employees for their efforts: employee lunches (even potluck lunches), cake and coffee, cookouts, and gift certificates are great ways to recognize employees for a job well done.

38

Have a budget for small cash awards.

Cash awards are a great way to motivate and reward, and employees love them. Even small amounts ($50, $100) will be a big hit. Plan for this amount as you develop this year's budget.

39

Try to identify performance roadblocks immediately.

Pay close attention to employee performance so that you can address any problems immediately. It will be easier to identify the cause of the substandard performance and identify specific actions necessary to improve it. Don't put off this needed diagnosis: It will create a much more effective work environment for everybody.

40

Develop a budget for employee training.

As you plan for next year's budget, include dollars that can be used for employee training. Figure five days of training for every full-time employee; have your training department help you come up with the cost of an average day of training.

41

Identify training opportunities in your company.

If your company is large, you might already have an in-house staff of training professionals and specific training courses available to employees. Find out what's available and the details (when, where, at what time, and necessary prerequisites). Then get your employees signed up.

42

Create workshops for common training needs.

An in-house training department can be invaluable when it comes to creating training experiences for unique needs in your employee group. Identify an individual who is able to help you clarify the needs, desired outcomes, and the learning process that will address employees' need for training.

43

Use employees as training consultants.

If you have in-house "experts" in a given area of performance, use them! You will be able to develop your employees inexpensively, build teamwork, and address the deficiencies in a much more timely manner.

44

Determine strengths and weaknesses.

What are the overall factors that contribute to your team's success or failure? How is your team performing relative to those factors? Where are you performing best? Where does the team need to improve significantly? Get some hard data on your team, and develop a plan to address what you find.

45

Organize workshops based on common needs.

Once you've diagnosed the needs of your team, it should be easy to identify common training needs among those who work for you. As you plan to address these deficiencies, group your employees together. They will enjoy the training and it will be easier to do follow-up and reinforcement once the training is completed.

46

Identify your team's key processes.

Processes tend to drive results. How does work get done? How does work flow from one point to another? Where are the bottlenecks? As you identify and improve the processes, you will improve the overall performance of your team's work.

47

Spend frequent time with your employees.

You need to see them in action. Be sure that what they are doing is in keeping with your performance expectations. Where are the bottlenecks? What can be done better? Who demonstrates a high level of skill that needs to be reproduced in others? Whose performance needs significant improvement?

48

Make notes about your performance observations.

Every time you observe your team going about its work, make a mental note of what you see. Who's not working collaboratively? Who's emerging as a leader? What is slowing them down (or revving them up)? Write down what you conclude and put these notes in the employees' drop files (remember them?).

49

Schedule appraisals 7 to 10 days before the event.

Inform your employees of the date and time of each appraisal, and be sure to give ample notification so that they can gather their thoughts about their performance over the previous year. You should also give them the opportunity to formulate questions regarding their present performance, as well as their potential.

Pick a neutral location for the appraisal.

Choose a conference room rather than your office for the appraisal meeting. You want to present the meeting as an opportunity for dialogue and exchange, rather than as a situation where the employee is being "called on the carpet."

51

Prepare a written summary of the employee's work.

Note performance strengths as well as areas for improvement, and request feedback and input from others. Does the document sound like you've done a fair job of assessing the employee's strengths and weaknesses? Or does it look as if you have an axe to grind? Does the feedback reflect the entire year, rather than just the past few weeks? Then write and re-write the summary until it's perfect.

52

Note specific examples of performance strengths and weaknesses in your summary.

This should be relatively easy if you have been using a drop file. Be as specific as possible, noting date, event, and any feedback you received from other people.

53

Make sure the appraisal looks professional.

The appraisal should be typewritten, but handwritten appraisals are fine IF the handwriting is totally legible and you use black ink (this is best for photocopying). Your company might have an online appraisal document; if it does, make sure you proofread it and run spell check before you print it out. Make a copy for your own records, and be sure to date it.

54

Review the written appraisal with the employee's supervisor.

Ask the supervisor their perspective on the employee's performance. What has he or she observed about the employee that would be relevant for inclusion in the appraisal? If it is your organization's practice, have your supervisor sign the completed appraisal.

55

Plan at least 60 minutes for the appraisal.

The employee appraisal usually covers a significant period of time (typically a year) and is intended to look at the past (what you've done) and the future (what you can or should do in the future). There will be a significant amount of information to cover, so allow plenty of time.

56

Plan the appraisal meeting.

Make sure you will not be doing all of the talking. Consider dividing the time up by starting with a summary of the year (which is typically all that employees are listening for). Then follow that statement with feedback about the first part of the performance period, the middle part of the performance period, and then the end of the performance period. Reinforce the summary of the year (i.e., "As a result of all that we've just reviewed, I see your performance as being _____ for the year."). After this, discuss the employee's developmental needs and plans for the future.

57

Ask the employee to identify what went well.

Focus on this performance period in the appraisal. After you give the employee ample time to discuss these performance strengths, you as supervisor should share additional information that supports your assessment.

58

Ask the employee to be ready to discuss performance.

If you give the employee plenty of advance notification of the appraisal, the appraisal meeting is more likely to become a productive dialogue about what you each consider to be performance strengths, weaknesses, and areas that need some focus.

Ask the
employee to
come with
written notes.

Encourage employees to write down their own assessments and conclusions about how they're doing. This is a good way of training them to be their own performance improvement consultants. You will also make your job much easier, since the employee will be able to come to the appraisal discussion with information in hand.

During the Appraisal

One of the most difficult tasks for any supervisor is the performance appraisal itself. There are many reasons why supervisors dislike appraisals:

- It's difficult to give bad news.
- It's difficult to give good news.
- The supervisor is not comfortable with confrontation—especially if the employee is surprised.
- The employee might not like what she or he hears.
- The employee, if receiving positive feedback, might expect significant financial rewards or promotions that are not presently available.

All of these concerns and issues can be overcome if the supervisor plans and manages the appraisal meeting.

Begin by thinking about the appraisal as a conversation or dialogue about the employee's performance. Maintain that perspective throughout the appraisal meeting.

Remember that the appraisal meeting is a dialogue. Welcome the employee's input, but do not abandon your agenda for the meeting. Your goal should be to create a collaborative conversation about the employee's performance that will lead to joint commitments.

Bring the completed appraisal to the meeting.

Your completed appraisal should reflect good, balanced feedback on the employee's performance, and it should be reviewed by your supervisor. If your supervisor provided you with suggestions for improvement, be sure they are reflected in the appraisal as well.

61

Bring your drop file, along with specific examples.

If you've done a consistent job of maintaining the drop file, you should have multiple examples of good and bad performance that have been gathered throughout the year. You might have to answer questions regarding points contained in your appraisal document; having the documentation available will help you and your employee see this situation from a common perspective.

62

Set a comfortable, conversational tone.

Begin by talking about an area of common interest (i.e., family, sports, art, music, outside interests) or a topic relative to your company or department. Make sure the conversation is comfortable and that the employee is at ease, despite the nature of the meeting.

63

Review the purpose of the appraisal meeting.

A natural question for the employee might be "Why are we here?" so begin by explaining the purpose of the meeting. In general, your purpose is to look at the employee's performance over the past year and identify those areas that went well and the areas that didn't go as well as you hoped. In addition, you should identify goals and objectives for the next year's performance.

64

Tell the employee how long the meeting will be.

Many employees approach a performance appraisal as if they are about to have a root canal. Provide them with information on how long the meeting will last; this at least keeps them from sitting on the edge of their seats and losing their focus. An hour should be more than adequate for this meeting.

Ask the employee what he or she would like to get out of the meeting.

What would the employee like to know? What would he or she like you to know as a result of this meeting? Start with the employee's needs and expectations; this helps to set the expectation that the meeting will satisfy both of your needs—not just yours as the supervisor.

Clarify the meeting's purpose.

Performance appraisals tend to be stressful for everyone. Even though you might have told the employee why you're doing an appraisal, reinforce the purpose in the meeting. People do forget—especially when undergoing a level of stress or discomfort.

67

Clarify the direction of the meeting.

Think about using a statement such as "Here's how I would like us to use our time…." Then describe the general direction of the meeting (i.e., "I'd like for us to start by taking a look at the things that went well this past year. I'll ask you to begin, and I'll fill in what you might have missed. Then, we'll look at the other side of your performance.")

68

Ask the employee to summarize the year.

Many employees have already made well-developed and highly objective assessments of their own performance. That can make your job that much easier. Allow such an employee time to voice his or her opinion without interrupting or correcting them. When the employee has finished, let them know that you would like to share some thoughts.

Add any short comments that might lend additional perspective.

This part of the appraisal meeting should focus on framing the performance year. Overall, was the year a strong one? A weak one? Or a mixed one? Save the details of the performance year for later in the appraisal conversation.

70

Ask the employee to identify the things that went well.

Ask for specific examples. Do not allow the employee to make blanket statements such as, "It was an okay year." Ask for details: "What made the year an okay one?" "What were the projects that you felt good about?"

71

Do not rush reviewing the employee's accomplishments.

It is important that the employee feel good about his or her accomplishments. It is this feeling of success that will be built on as you look at the areas where the employee's performance could be improved. Therefore, when reviewing the employee's strengths and achievements, point out specific positive examples, be sincere, and do not rush.

72

Accentuate the positive.

Some employees are reluctant to share their positive results for fear of appearing overly proud or boastful. Be generous with any additional thoughts you have about the employee's positive achievements over the previous performance year.

73

Share the comments other people have made.

If you have received positive comments from others relative to the employee's performance, share them at this point in the appraisal conversation. As much as possible, try to represent the comments of others accurately so that the employee has a full appreciation of the feedback.

74

Clarify and reinforce the impact of their performance.

As you review these positive events with your employee, make sure he or she understands the impact of his or her actions. The things individuals do can get lost in the many moving pieces of the company. Make sure the employee understands how customers, the company, your department, and their peers have benefited from their actions and achievements.

75

Have an active dialogue.

Managers tend to create "a talk show" performance appraisal, where the supervisor asks questions and the employee gives answers. Avoid this! Instead, offer your perspective on specific areas of the employee's performance. He or she will be able to compare their own perspective on what they did with the perspectives of others (yours and those who have provided feedback).

76

Do not rush through the appraisal.

Allow time for the employee to reflect on what has gone well. This might be one of the few opportunities the employee will have to really consider what he or she has accomplished and the impact of those accomplishments. Taking the time to reflect on these positive outcomes is much like taking the time to "cool down" after a lengthy workout.

77

Be willing to modify the appraisal.

The employee might identify significant results or contributions that you failed to include in your appraisal. If the situation warrants, modify the appraisal to include this new information. You will reinforce the notion that you and the employee are working together to produce top-flight performance.

78

Close this section of the appraisal discussion by summarizing the strengths.

The purpose here is to provide a summary statement regarding these significant events. Closure also provides yet another opportunity to reinforce the positive results the employee has achieved during this performance period.

79

Build on the positive results during the next stage.

So much of positive change lies in identifying what one does well and leveraging that strength to affect the areas of performance that need improvement. As you think about the next area of focus in the appraisal, recall the strengths. Don't toss them out the window! Avoid statements like "Now on to the bad news" since the intent of the appraisal is not to offer bad news, but to continue to discuss *what is* in order to identify ways of making it even better.

Ask the employee to focus on things they would do differently.

If the employee could do the current year over, what would they do differently? Avoid the tendency to focus on a message that sounds like, "Here are the many things you screwed up." As much as possible, focus on diagnosis, not the delivery of negative messages. Be sure to give them time to reflect before they respond.

81

Remember that the focus is on learning.

Emphasize the things that the employee learned as a result of their negative experiences. This puts the focus not on the "flop," but on what the employee learned about the flop that would produce different outcomes in future attempts. Ask questions such as, "Knowing now what you didn't know at that point, what would you do differently?" or "Since hindsight is usually 20/20, what would you do differently now?"

82

Allow time for the employee to consider what they would do differently.

It is startling how often we forget to reflect on our past actions. Many people shy away from "armchair quarterbacking," but ask the employee to do it anyway. Top performers improve because they continually analyze what they do in order to identify improvement opportunities.

83

Add your comments to the conversation.

Make your comments as specific as possible by citing events, dates, times, and persons involved. In many ways, you and the employee are building a collective memory of the year. By sharing your respective data and perspectives, you are creating a far more accurate picture of the year than either of you could have created alone.

84

Include feedback from others.

You shared positive feedback. Now be sure to include critical comments from peers, customers, your boss, other groups, and co-workers that are relevant to the area of performance improvement.

85

Avoid non-productive "hammering."

Be careful not to repeat the same criticisms over and over again. There will be areas where the performance was not as strong as expected. The goal of the dialogue in this part of the appraisal should focus on *developing the employee's understanding* of what he or she did and how it could have been done better. When the employee understands what he or she could have done better or differently and he or she seems committed to doing that, move on.

86

Make sure the employee understands the "so what."

It is important that you help the employee understand the implications of his or her behavior. For instance, you can say, "Here are some of the effects or repercussions of the things that did not go well for you last year…"

87

Recognize the employee's different perspective.

It is totally possible that the employee will not see a given area of performance the same way you do. He or she might not consider the impact to be as significant as what you noted. Rather than shut the employee off, hear them out. You do not have to immediately change your perspective, but it might be of great value to understand the point she or he is making.

88

Recognize that the buck stops with you.

The company ultimately holds YOU responsible for the employee's performance. Input from other people is valuable, but you are the one who must make the final assessment regarding the employee's performance. As harsh as this may seem, the management of employee performance is not a situation where everyone has equal votes.

89

Close with a summary statement.

A summary statement outlines the significant gaps in the employee's performance that he or she should focus on in order to become an even stronger performer during the next performance period. Identify these and make sure that you and the employee agree on them. If the employee disagrees about what you believe are weak areas, recognize that you are ultimately responsible for the team's results.

Ask for the employee's ideas regarding performance improvement.

If the employee has done his or her homework before the meeting, he or she will have ideas about how to improve performance. Review that list and add those things that emerged during the appraisal discussion.

91

Note the most important development needs.

As you review the list of development actions, note those things that you think are the most important. The priority ranking might be based on present deficiency, but it might also be based on company goals and objectives, which can make a particular area of performance of greater importance than another at the present time. Whatever criteria you use to determine importance, make sure that the employee has a sense of the priority order for their actions.

92

Offer additional performance suggestions.

Your perspective as the supervisor will be useful in determining additional areas on which the employee should focus. Don't be reluctant to express what you think. As the employee's coach, your job is to ensure top-notch performance. Your suggestions will be important in moving performance in a more positive direction.

93

Use several strategies for skill development.

There are several ways to go about improving performance:

- Monitor another individual's performance (live or by video) and comment on the things that he or she did that your employee could try.
- Arrange for real-time performance coaching from someone who performs a particular skill well.

- Check out the latest books on the subject and note the actions that the employee might do differently.
- Attend a workshop that focuses on the needed skills and develop action plans to integrate the new skills into the employee's performance.
- Observe someone (live or by video) performing the skill poorly so that you both can talk about how the skill could have been better performed.

Start with a few of these strategies to improve performance.

94

Agree on the Action Plan.

Develop an Action Plan form to set and record the details, including the dates by which the development activities should be accomplished. Make sure that you and the employee each have a copy of this development agreement to demonstrate your mutual commitment to the outcomes.

95

Determine what resources will be needed.

Make sure you are clear on what the employee needs from you as supervisor in order to get started on his or her development plans. If you know this up front, you can obtain the financing (if necessary) or make time or resources available to support the employee's development actions.

96

Identify specific resources that will be necessary.

Make sure you understand the employee's plan to improve his or her performance. If the employee has identified specific resources (money, people, or other resources), make sure you know what they are and can provide them. If you cannot, make the necessary changes in the plan immediately, rather than waste time on a plan that will not happen.

97

Summarize the developmental actions.

The summary is simply another way of creating joint commitment to the path forward. Make sure you and the employee are on the same path. Many a disaster has been created by the employee taking one route, while the supervisor is assuming another. You and the employee must both understand what is doing to be done, why it is being done, when it is going to be done, where it will be done, and by whom it will be done.

98

Sign the performance appraisal document.

If you have not already done so, sign and date the appraisal document. If modifications are necessary to the appraisal (based on new data you received), make those modifications and then sign the final appraisal.

Request the employee's signature.

In most companies, the employee's signature is necessary to attest to the fact that the appraisal has been reviewed with him or her. It is usually not designed to indicate that the employee is in full agreement with the contents of the appraisal. If the employee disagrees with some or all of what is written, request their signature, but suggest that they write a brief statement such as, "I have reviewed this appraisal, but do not agree with the content." This is a reasonable way to help the employee to go on record as disagreeing with the appraisal's content.

After the Appraisal

If you have made it to this point in the performance management process, you have covered a good deal of ground. You have set goals with the employee, reviewed the employee's performance against those goals, provided periodic feedback on the employee's performance (in an effort to encourage consistently high performance), and done an appraisal that reflects the employee's performance and the impact of that performance on the organization over a specific period of time.

After the appraisal discussion, focus on addressing the improvement areas identified in the appraisal. These improvement areas can include things that the employee will need to do more of, things that the employee should do less of, and things that the employee should continue to do as she or he has done in the past.

During this after-appraisal period, your task is to monitor the commitments made during the appraisal conversation and make sure that the employee is working on these areas in a focused fashion. It is important that you identify the actions that you as supervisor must do to support the employee's performance improvement efforts.

Make sure *you* are not the roadblock in the employee's performance improvement efforts.

100

Follow up on every appraisal commitment.

An easy way to follow up is to put performance improvement goals on your calendar (paper or electronic). If you have these follow-up dates on your calendar, you will be able to keep track of the commitments made and hold up your end of the partnership created to improve the employee's performance.

101

Look for opportunities to celebrate.

Numerous opportunities exist to celebrate changes in performance and acknowledge individual and department achievement. Celebrations provide additional energy for the level of challenges that need to be addressed. Imagine that your team consists of long-distance runners: At various intervals, your goal will be to cheer them on, give them water, and offer "pep talks" to keep them focused on what they have achieved and what lies ahead of them. Celebrate often!

And When You Think You Are Finished...

One way to think about performance management is to compare it to improving our
health.

Some individuals take care of their health needs
by playing team sports. Even though they are in
terrible physical shape as a result of poor diet and
poor exercise habits, they join a soccer, softball, or
basketball team in the hope that they will be able
to shock their systems back into shape. This is, all
too often, the way managers approach the appraisal process: They shock themselves into creating appraisals by locking themselves in their offices
a few days before appraisals are due and cranking
them out.

Not good.

A more reasonable approach (and less
painful—really!) is to pay as much ongoing atten-

tion to issues of employee performance as those who seriously workout pay to their health. If you pay regular and close attention to employee performance, you will not have to worry about system breakdowns or other distresses that occur because you failed to pay ongoing attention to this critical area.

Do not become a performance couch potato.

102

Start this book all over again.

The ideas in this book can be used again and again. Go through them step-by-step and you will find that they will become a natural part of the work that you do. Your employees will be better able to manage their own performance because you have given them tools, techniques, and approaches for doing so.

103

Give this book to a colleague who needs it.

Performance management and performance improvement are part of the agenda of most of today's corporate leaders. If you know of someone who could use a few ways to help employees perform better (or organizations perform better), buy them a copy of this book.

They will be glad you did—and so will we.